SOAP

A Cleansing of the Soul and
a Bath of Self-Realization

ALEXIS MONIQUE

SOAP

A Cleansing of the Soul and a Bath of Self-Realization

ALEXIS MONIQUE

SOAP: A Cleansing of the Soul and a Bath of Self-Realization

Revision Publishing LLC books may be purchased for educational, business, or sales promotional use. For information, please email contact@revisionpub.com or visit www.revisionpub.com.

First edition

Library of Congress Control Number: 2025414067

SOAP: A Cleansing of the Soul and a Bath of Self-Realization / Alexis Monique - 1.) POE024000 - POETRY / Women Authors 2.) POE023080 - POETRY / Subjects & Themes / Motivational & Inspirational 3.) SEL045000 - SELF-HELP / Journaling.

ISBN 979-8-9929944-9-0 (paperback)
ISBN 979-8-9936608-3-7 (hardcover)

Editing by Lauren Savage
Photography by Terry Thomas
Digital Illustrations by Amaya Thomas
Cover/Interior Design by Samia Asif
Photography © 2026 by Terry Thomas. All photographs in this collection are by Terry Thomas, and used with the photographer's permission.
Digital illustrations © 2026 by Amaya Thomas. All digital illustrations in this collection are by Amaya Thomas, and used with the artist's permission.

Table of Contents

PREFACE

I wrote this book to inspire women to break free from barriers—both societal and self-imposed. A few years ago, I found myself in a difficult space, mourning the loss of several loved ones. I began to feel my spirit slowly unravel. Then I reached a pivotal moment: I was diagnosed with breast cancer and underwent four surgeries and a course of radiation within a single year.

Through it all, I clung to the Creator for strength. The more I spoke to God, the more I pondered my purpose. As I searched my soul, I realized that I had neglected many parts of my identity. I had lost sight of my individuality and the things that once made me feel alive.

Outside of my roles as a wife, mother, and businesswoman, there was little to nothing left. Like so many women, I had given up many of the things that made me, *me*. This book is a reclamation of self, giving the poet inside an unapologetic voice. It is a nod to the multifaceted roles and identities that women embody.

I named this book *SOAP* because it is meant to wash away any preconceived notions about how women should show up in the world. It is an invitation to live boldly, beyond stereotypes, and embrace the fullness of your own truth. At its heart, this book is a tribute and a word of encouragement.

DEDICATION

Dear *Ymaya* and *Isaac*,

My prayer is that you continue to feed your souls through your unique, individual passions. I encourage you to live life fully present, finding fulfillment in each moment. Pursue your purpose boldly, wholeheartedly, and without fear of change. You are both creatives in your own right, blessed with many talents. Continue to explore the things that bring you peace. May you live out your dreams with pride, personality, grace, and power!

You are, equally and entirely, my absolute proudest creations—art manifested from my womb, which God so graciously allowed me to carry. The Savior favored me again by allowing me to raise your beautiful spirits. Thank you for your hearts, filled with love, that have been monumental parts of my life. I hope that you enjoy this book, and it makes you proud.

All my love,
Mom

Chapter I:
POSITIVE BODY IMAGE

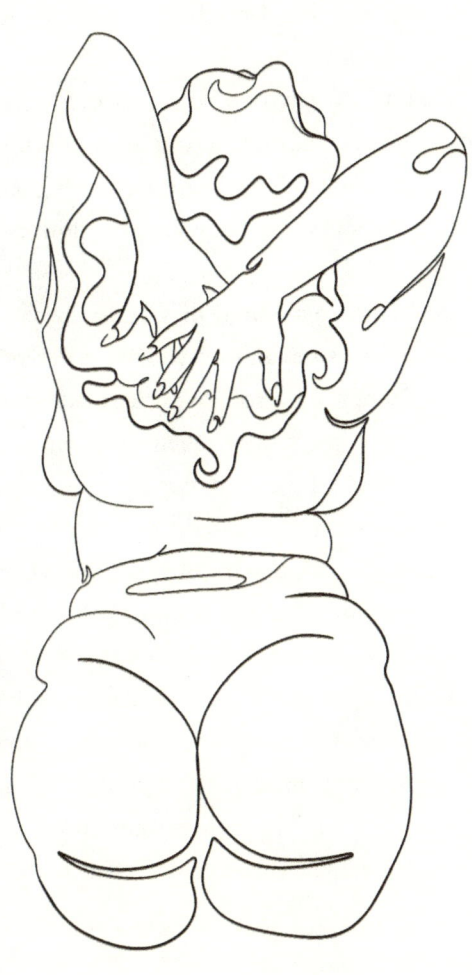

SOAP

The early morning is a sacred space because I get to wash this face.
As I apply my cleanser, I work to render and restore,
to replace this drywall cover and recover from
what's been hiding under my pores.
A good lather ensures that deep cleanse that I've been chasing after.

As I pat my face dry, I close my eyes, unwind,
and apply my vitamin C serum in an upward motion,
followed up with a healthy dose of loving sensations,
coaxing my mind away from any lingering doubts or limitations.

In deep meditation, I begin my day
with an ample spray of moisturizing sun block lotion.
Then, I begin rolling my iced jade stone
over all of my swollen facial zones,
mapping and massaging the areas
where stress has created a home in my body.
Carefully spotting any traces of puffiness left behind,
restoring my mind, using this *me* time to find healing.

Last night's cry is just proof that I'm in tune with my feelings—
revealing the brightness of today's glow.
As my face shimmers with glimmers of hope,
I find it absolutely amazing
what you can do with a little soap.

MY SPIRITUAL
Light

To my arms, I hope you know I meant you no harm
when I covered you, not to keep you warm,
but so that others wouldn't be alarmed by your flab.

To my belly, I apologize for the comparison to jelly
and for steadily covering you up.
I shouldn't have crammed you into bodysuits.
I should have embraced you, freed you, and let you loose.

To my caboose, my wide ass,
forgive me for pulling you in as others walked past,
instead of allowing you to sway with sass.
You are an asset: a cushioned pallet, packed and stacked up with love.

To my love handles, I should have handled your pleas to be free,
but instead I was ashamed.
When you bared yourself through my shirt,
I filled you with blame and found another top
to put a stop to your existence.
I told you that you were better off hidden
and made you friends with shame.

To every pound that I gained, I should have embraced you
instead of being embarrassed,
for you bear witness to the blessings of Christ.
I was given more than enough food to fill my appetite.
My negative attitude towards you just wasn't right.

To my cellulite, I apologize for all of the criticism and creams—
for trying to alter your appearance to make you seem smooth.
I'm sorry for becoming so consumed
that I covered you up only to overheat my legs during summer months.

To my body, I apologize for robbing you of all of your glory.
When you could have shut down, you stayed around for me.
Surely, you deserve the best.
You are my sanctuary, a vessel for me to live and attain rest.

You have been gracious despite my negative statements.
You are a gift of actualization.
Please forgive me for not treating you right.
To my body, thank you for housing my spiritual light.

BISCUITS AND
Big Backs

Baking biscuits by the stacks,
reflected in my backside, buttered, wide, and thick.
I'll be wrapping all of it in gratefulness
as I round out the edges of this perfect peach frame,
I'll commence squeezing, and love-handling every pound that I gain.

I can't complain; embracing this frame
is a perfect piece of heaven.
We have to stop associating big backs
with anything negative.
We have to change our perspective.

We are the same delicate women,
sticking to society's stomach,
powdered around the sides of our baskets,
emboldened, not trying to hide our soft sides.

We are fly, giving big backs a positive connotation,
claiming it as an affirmation.
The phrase "big back" is rolled in luxury—
a woman who provides good company,
the pure definition of comforting,
made entirely from scratch,
naturally packed with pounds of sexy,
a delicious recipe deserving of its name.

More and more seasoned with each pound that I gain,
my vision remains unchanged.
I still see myself the same and never complain about the
sacred work of maintaining this voluptuous frame—
all is the same in my heart.

So as I scarf down this bread,
I'm never worried about how the weight might spread.
I can shamelessly stretch this wide body out across the bed
because I am fixated and led by internal fires that need to be fed.

I can relax this big back
while I lay back my head.
I'll keep my self-esteem intact.
There are no spaces of lack or lust;
because I remain in touch with and trust this body.
I'm in deep appreciation for the time that it's gotten me through.
This dough has rolled me right into this stage of life.

The scent of contentment smells nice.
I'll keep baking creating a temperature rise,
and remain in deep admiration of my thunder thighs,
high off this warm supply of country biscuits.

What a delicacy I have gotten to witness, evolve, and plate.
I will continue to appreciate my loaded stack,
pulled fresh from the oven rack,
packed with flavor.
From now on, you can catch me indulging in every layer,
savoring my big back and biscuits.

Society often devalues women as we age and our bodies change, but we can choose to draw from our experiences, extract wisdom, and lean into our power. Take a moment to reflect on the ways your body has carried and blessed you through time. Celebrate the changes and functions that have sustained you over the years.

Use the space below to express gratitude for each part of your body and for the life stages that have shaped who you are. You might start with quiet meditation before writing—whatever feels right for you.

If it's hard to see beauty in your body today, try to notice one small way it serves you. The way that we see ourselves is a manifestation of our thoughts. Clean your lenses, look with compassionate eyes, and remember to use soap.

_____

_____

_____

_____

_____

_____

_____

_____

_____

_____

_____

_____

Chapter II:
BODILY ATTUNEMENT

OCTOBER

I don't know how to feel, but I know I felt a lump. I also feel like calling the hospital might be a little too much. I know that my breast tissue is tough, and I don't want them unnecessarily examining stuff.

Plus, going in could be rough because I'll likely walk out of the doctor's office with a bunch of anxiety. So, before I let them determine what may be going on inside of me, I visited Mom's house.

I trust her judgment without a shadow of a doubt, so I unbuttoned my blouse and asked for her opinion. She immediately confirmed what I had been feeling and demanded that I schedule an appointment as soon as possible at the medical building. I was inclined to listen—something in my intuition was urging me to be seen.

Things quickly began to evolve. I found myself going through the motions, and taking time off from my job, my schedule grew clogged with doctor's visits. The cellular abnormality was no longer hidden. I tried to come to grips with this new reality, doing my best not to freeze in shock by how it all was sounding.

Instead, I focused on deliberately listening to the physicians' specific descriptions of my condition. They were efficient and began to pivot toward further examinations to determine whether the growth formation was benign or malignant.

Stuck in this uncomfortable position, I did my best to submerge the fearful feelings while awaiting the biopsy results to learn exactly what I was facing.

The procedures were only half of it; now I had to wait. And when the results finally came in, I had to manage my mental state.

It's kinda hard to wrap your mind around a disease when your body feels great. Before too long, I was given a surgery date and a treatment plan. I felt encouraged that I would land on my feet. Allowing my faith to guide me, I turned to the God residing in me for strength when I hit the peaks of my anxiety. Still, pain grew inside of me as I witnessed how hard other women were fighting.

This story isn't the easiest to tell, but it needed to be told. It's important for people to recognize the early signs. So with this in mind, if you feel a lump or notice discharge, discoloration, or any other unusual changes to your breast shape or nipples, please remember how critical it is to be seen immediately. More time allows more opportunity for the infectious cells to spread.

My hope is that you are not frightened by what you've read. Instead, my intention is to spread awareness and inspire you to participate in regular self and medical breast exams—to stay attuned to your body, and on top of your mammograms.

Early detection of cancer greatly increases survival rates. I share this as a survivor blessed enough to advocate through my survival story.

THE BLUEPRINT
of a Woman

I hate to complain about my bodily functions. It sounds like I'm not one with my womanhood, as if I'm disregarding our ability to create the luscious garden of life. However, after suffering several strikes to my body, strife has created wounds.

The blueprint is signified by the bruises we endure as we experience our cycles. It is a means of survival, traced in the color red—an outline of sorts to maintain a level head as we dread Aunt Flow's visit.

She always feels permitted to overstay her welcome, arriving with several friends—the ones that mend themselves to your womb, consuming themselves in your reproductive business. An invite was never extended, yet they stay!

Benign tumors composed of fibrous muscle tissue get in the way, causing issues within your anatomy. As the crowd grows, the heavier the blood flows, saturating tampons and extra-long maxi pads, staining my clothes.

Think of them as the ovulation family, who knows no bounds, sticks around and wreaks havoc. Always drastically disturbing the peace, dirtying up bed sheets, sitting in the creases of panties, never discreet with their meddling, leaving you wailing in pain.

It's a relentless game of survival, trying birth control to get a hold of your hormones, taking vitamins to enter into normal pH zones, grabbing hold of heating pads hoping the heat outlasts the cramps.

I am determined not to let this internal fire spread, causing severe migraines in my head. These forces proceeded ahead to conspire and create more of a strain throughout my body. The pain feels ungodly. Why ought we be ashamed when Ms. Menstrual has drained our blood, iron, and energy?

Habitually waging war inside the anatomy of my feminine frame. I tamed some weight gain by avoiding harmful foods that I craved; alleviating the salt that actively inflamed my body. However, this only got me so far.

Enticed by light exercise thinking my endorphins would rise, until I finally realized that none of it was working. I freed myself permanently when I saw a doctor. My impostors were spotted, and although I've now parted with my womb, I've cheerfully welcomed this new beautiful blueprint!

Please excuse the bloodshed in the last poem, but it reflects a reality that many women experience and rarely talk about. Fibroids are very common among women of color. Breast cancer in particular is also prevalent in our communities. There are many factors—such as the environment, genetics, and lack of accessibility to health care—that you can't control, so it's important to focus on what you can.

Stay mindful of your body's signals, evaluate them, and respond with care. Listening to the messages that our bodies send is a vital part of preventative health. Nurture your well-being through healthy habits, self-advocacy, and regular checkups.

Write a personal vow to yourself to stay in tune with your body. Don't be afraid to explore and examine it. Remember, early detection saves lives, and you know your body best because you live inside of it.

_____

_____

_____

_____

_____

_____

_____

_____

_____

_____

Chapter III:
SELF-HELP

SELF-
Care

To lie in front of a fan and feel the palpitations of the wind massage my ass.

To pour myself a flute of crisp, chilled, white wine and top the hell off of the glass.

To saunter to the tub with therapeutic oils for a self-administered foot rub.

To hear the sound of smooth jazz play in the background as I ease this voluptuous body down into a warm lavender-scented bubble bath.

To adorn my crown and ground myself.

To walk barefoot through the sand or grass allowing every step to flow fluidly, moving me spiritually and feeding my soul.

To meditate and unwind, to keep zero track of time and give space for my mind to wander or reminisce on the sweet kiss of sunshine against this magnificently magical melanin goldmine.

To stare in the mirror as I brush through this thick kinky brown hair in administration of self while praising God for good health.

I am wealthy, in love with plenty of riches to share.

As I speak my affirmations, I declare that each and every day I will find a new way to cultivate this journey of self-care.

I pray that my poem encourages you all to do the same.

GRATITUDE

Over the years, our gratitude evolves.
Just as we grow, shift jobs, and twist the doorknobs of new opportunities.
The more we realize that blessings don't originate from us exclusively,
we intuitively gain more of an appreciation for life,
and for some, even a strengthened relationship with Christ.

I'm a faithful Christian and find myself exceedingly grateful
to fulfill God's vision for my life.
Till this day, I am still grateful for the lessons I've learned
despite the price.
I'm so grateful to still be in the race of life and
have substance despite my sacrifices.
I am grateful for silence, the stillness, the peace and quiet.
I am grateful for the timeless memories
and the plethora of sensory stimulations of love.
I am proud to know true sisterhood
that has held tight, kept me right, and encouraged me to rise above my troubles.
I'm blessed to have two children that I'm extremely
proud of—an indestructible bond.

The practice of gratitude has become a fond tradition,
gifted from God, grounding my thought posture.
It has been a doctor, treating the lenses in which I see.
It's an intentional mental shift
that brings clarity to our existence,
and helps us to continue on strong with persistence.
My heart is full and content with this immense gratitude.

Journal Exercise 3

Many women forget to be of service to themselves. We are natural nurturers, and it is necessary that we pour into ourselves. Administering self-help can take shape through self-care and gratitude. Shifting our attention towards gratitude has many benefits. It allows us to attract and embody more of the good we focus on and engage with.

Use the space below to give attention to the things in your life that you are grateful for and to define self-care in a way that fits your needs. On challenging days, revisit what you've written as a reminder to keep practicing self-care and gratitude.

_____

_____

_____

_____

_____

_____

_____

_____

_____

_____

_____

_____

_____

_____

Chapter IV:
SELF-AWARENESS

BLACK
Coffee

It's like inviting people over for coffee
and intentionally throwing out all the sugar, milk, and cream.
Then, when you recognize that people are disappointed,
you perceive their "no thank yous" as mean.

As you proceed to insist,
you spill drips of black coffee all over their clothes.
Unable to let go of the urge, you keep pushing,
trying to force others to stomach the substance that you serve.

The drips signify the bitterness of your words, and they stain,
you blame others instead of facing your own hurt and pain.
People don't want to desert you,
and they don't deserve to feel the residue of your unhealed
spaces because they risk being hurt, too.

I encourage you to seek therapy, do the work and focus on yourself.
This will prevent you from spilling coffee,
staining, and blaming everyone else.

Most importantly, the next time you invite folks over for coffee,
you'll have milk, cream, and sugar out on the shelf!

SELECTIVE
Hearing

My hearing is not impaired—it's just selective.
I choose the words that will mesh well with my emotional digestion.
Those are the things I listen to.
I have ignored more than a few.

But my ability to aggressively deter unwelcome speech
attempting to reach my head have led me to satisfactory tokens of peace.
Instead of being provoked,
I'm actively revoking messages,
essentially protesting nonsense.

I consider this mental filtering,
a contraceptive that prohibits me from suffering.
So, instead of being reactive and focusing on recovery,
I've learned new ways of discovering proactive measures
to shield against the onslaught of verbal instigators
who have the urge to vomit.

I'm always scoping out new ways to stop this before it starts.
Only substantial words will be heard by my auditory receptive parts.

Most people want to be heard,
but those close to me have learned to adapt to my preference.
See, I prefer to witness the actionable sentiments,
something realistic that connects pure intentions.
That's the best way to get my attention.

I'm not good at listening to nonsense.
We all stand to benefit from clear communication.
My frustration is aimless conversation,
leaving discussions with no action plans set out to be taken,
just blatantly flooding my ears.
You see, I'm real, real selective about what I choose to hear.

ABSTINENCE

I refuse to be bruised by the images portrayed on the news.
All of the subliminal cues bleed classism, fascism, and division.
Racism is reflected through cryptic messaging on the television.
Thugs are described as those who choose activism,
the very souls who oppose systemic oppression.

Promoting social reflections of distorted ideals
with votes on the heels of presidential appeals.
There is blatant aggression towards acceptance.
Journalists have no neutrality,
shun intersectionality, and are undoubtedly biased,
promoting propaganda and popular trends
instead of feeding the souls of men.

Wrapped into this whirlwind of irresponsibility,
seeming trapped in the prism between capitalism and liberty,
I refuse to allow the "fake news" to consume me
or become glued, imprinted in my memory.

So, in order to see clearly,
I diligently guard my vision,
employ my intuition,
and abstain.

"Black Coffee" encourages readers to reflect on what they bring to the table while assessing what others are serving. "Selective Hearing" and "Abstinence" highlight the importance of knowing our mental limits and bring attention to the power of safeguarding our peace. We live in a society filled with constant noise and distractions, so I urge you to guard your mind and choose what truly serves you. We choose who and what we entertain. We can either accommodate chaos or choose to escort it out of our lives. Either way, it's a choice, and I pray that you choose yourself.

Try a house-cleaning exercise. Reflect on the people, habits, or thoughts that you can fast from or remove completely. Ask yourself: What purpose do they serve? Are they helpful or harmful to my mental health and spiritual growth? Write them below, and feel empowered to begin the process of washing away what no longer serves you.

_____

_____

_____

_____

_____

_____

_____

_____

_____

Chapter V:
SELF-ACTUALIZATION

THE
Rain

Calling on my subconscious after dark,
as my weakness begins to depart from hiding and my mind is spiraling,
it reminds me to be still—
not to rush my healing process. It will take time to come up off this depression.

I'm recollecting my biggest childhood lessons, the one in my head that said:
Little girl, I'ma need you to quit stressing, because baby, you can't afford to fall apart!
Don't you know there is an art to dealing with tremendous pain?
Go on, cry, but do it quietly tonight.
By sunlight, your eyes should be dried, and the only thing magnified should be your power!
You won't get far with a sour face.
Hold your head high and walk dignified. Be graceful.
After all, it is distasteful for you to facilitate a safe space.
Instead, I need you to save face and fix your posture.
I never asked you about your imposter syndrome.
All I know is, you've got to make it on your own. I've shown you resilience.
Deal with the hurt!
Only allow your composure to emerge.
And remember to submerge your soft side—
it will only magnify your chances of getting hurt.

These were the lessons that were projected from birth.
During my adolescence, as a form of protection,
I was taught to avert vulnerability—to put on my big girl panties,
portray the sweetness of candy, anything to avoid candidly facing
the underlying presence of pain.

I needed to remain in control; people couldn't know I struggled.
I had to shape shift, and attempt an unnatural facelift to create a quick illusion of
an energy shift, as I turned my frowns upside down.

Because I didn't understand, nor was I given permission to express big feelings,
it wasn't until I began healing that I learned the true power of dealing with discomfort—
that of revealing (the sometimes disgruntled woman) hidden under the pleasantries
of performative conformity.

I deserved the freedom of exposing the naked beauty that I had been withholding,
that authentic, raw appearance of me, wholly.

I needed to sit with the waves of emotions I had been holding and allow them to flow.
It is in these moments that you truly grow,
because you gain the experience to know
that you are more than capable of dealing with pain.

Sunshine is just as necessary as rain in the terrain of life.
I'm quite graced to be able to withstand and face the weather.
Nowadays, I'm standing in the rain without an umbrella.

MAKING

Space

I am grateful for your innocence,
that often transcends into resistance
from all of the bad that exists in the world.

I am grateful for the internal bliss
that kept you oblivious amid the chaos that you were surrounded with.
I am glad that you were able to protect yourself like this.

I appreciate escaping the darkness of the world
through the guise of your adolescent eyes—
for a mind that supplied me with creative expression,
providing an escape and revealing my landscape.
It created a map of me, for me, to explore
and to build an intimate connection with,
and truly become a knower of her.

I am grateful for the strength
I have been graced with through the past lessons,
and for the openness of your heart.
It remains the greatest part of our creation.
You were graced with free trust,
trust that never had to be earned.

You learned to forgive freely,
to provide a clean slate,
completely washing the plate of past incidents away.
You lived by these precious gifts long before you were touched by pain.
You will always remain my refuge for unconditional love.

You emit a strong hug of emotions,
some worn, torn, but still serve a purpose.
You are the clothes that shielded my naked heart,
you fold the garments of my broken parts with care.
You consist of rich, colorful layers of affection,
you smooth out all of my unpleasant thoughts,
ironing out the wrinkles in my mind.

You are the shield that withstood time
and protected me from harsh weather,
you mended me together,
warming my body and soul.

Your covering personifies
that best friend we all know.
It is because you showed me survival through sacrifice,
that I am able to recognize
the resilience of your fight.

I am learning not to villainize you for your plight.
I understand that, even with limited knowledge,
you only did what you thought was right.
I have no right to spite you.

I owe you an apology for silencing you,
hiding you, and denying you as a woman.
I appreciate that you did not break while I was in the making
and you were still becoming.
I apologize for shunning your mistakes,
and for not offering grace.
Truthfully, I'm grateful for your beauty
that extends beyond the echo of your grandmother's face,
and for space in your soul that holds God's power.

I wish that I was around to shower you
with the protection that you deserved,
to create a place you'd be heard,
and to be the living verb that love is.
I would have allowed you to be a kid,
let you live,
sure to give you time to grow up slow.
Little girl, I apologize most
for not recognizing your existence as an adult.

Dear, little girl who resides inside,
I'm sorry.
I honor your tenacity to survive.
From here on out, I'm keeping you alive.
There is enough room for us both to bloom and thrive.

I AM
a Woman

I am essential.
I am clothed.
I am the finest garment in your wardrobe.
I am colorful and bold—
behold my power.
I am a warrior and possess superpowers.
I am female, every second, every moment, every hour.
I devour the hate beneath me.
I am protected by God and crafted uniquely.
I devote myself to the universe completely.
Fertility is distinct within the makeup of me—I am Divine.
I am a woman, I am beautiful, I am sublime and fine.
Designed with arches and curves,
The Creator's perfect artwork.
Ladies first, because we elevate, alleviate pain, we
soothe cries, nurture, and brighten eyes.
We are soul ties and deeply connected.
Although men and women are closely intersected,
women are the earth's most vital possession because we bear life.
Your endorphins rise as we pleasure your eyes.
The world fully lies on our shoulders.
Women are the strong boulders of society.
Undeniably, we are your loud conscience, even when your vices try to quiet me.
We are sweet and spicy.
We sip from the same glasses that raise as we walk past.
Red carpets roll out fast beneath our feet—
all hail reign to the queens with tilted crowns
and gold things gripping to their teeth!

REACH

We are always reaching, aren't we?
Even those hardly making headway
are steadfast in prying their way to what's next.
What an obsession—
to glance right over the blessing of now,
eager to reach over to the next milestone,
mistaking time as our own.

I'm not suggesting that we find complacency in our homes;
I just find rushing moments wrong.
We can't get back those good times once they're gone.
We need to honor our immediate space before moving on.

To reach is to seek.
However, greeting the present imparts lessons to savor—
multidimensional layers and mental keepsakes
that benefit us later.

It's all about finding favor in today,
and I believe this is the best way to reach.

This chapter invites self-discovery. "The Rain" expresses the power of embracing everything that influences the makeup of individuals. "I Am a Woman" celebrates the liberation of being your authentic self, outside of the restraints of conformity. It is about embodying the fullness of womanhood. "Reach" teaches us to slow down, appreciate the present, and honor the women we're becoming. Together, these poems call us to see ourselves clearly and love what we find in the reflection, symbolic to the mirror illustrated in the beginning of this chapter.

Take a moment to describe the woman you strive to be—the one who lives inside you, whom you sometimes quiet or suppress. She deserves expression, acceptance, and the freedom to live out loud. Reflect on who you are today, the lessons that shaped you, and the grace you owe yourself along the way. Meet the woman in the mirror and honor her with your words.

_____

_____

_____

_____

_____

_____

_____

_____

_____

_____

_____

Chapter VI:
SELF-REGULATION

THE DANGER
of Silence

Sis, value the voice you've got,
because saying what you mean says a whole hell of a lot.
It's in opposition of what was taught
to be a woman's position but sis, I need you to speak.
Stating your piece generates a huge release—
an act of advocacy I'm practicing myself.

Words, I won't shy away from;
instead, I'll embrace them and release them
where and when they need to be felt.
You might not appreciate the landing,
but this courage took planning,
and how will I generate understanding
if I keep my mouth shut?
I have something on my spirit;
I am regurgitating from the gut.
I need you to hear it.
This is my truth—come near it.

Not until you revive my cry
and validate my feelings can I soften.
Far too often, my intentions fail
because you refuse to hear me unless I yell.
Locked in a cell of my own pain,
but if once, when I call your name,
you'd remain tame, let me explain,
and be attentive.
Sit down, you're alpha, and stop being defensive.

If you were to listen,
I might just learn how to be submissive.

So next time, instead of being dismissive,
embrace what's on my mind.
Be someone I can rely on,
and a shoulder I can cry on.

I will not be reduced to hiding from my emotions.
I'm done with commotions
created behind words never stated.
I am no longer quieting myself.
I will speak loud and let my words resound,
no more muffled sounds
or talking out loud to walls.
No longer accepting social protocols,
I'm standing tall on my words once and for all.
There will be no retainer,
because you can't restrain my thoughts.

One of the most valuable lessons ever taught,
the reason my tongue won't get caught—
Freedom of speech has been long fought.
So free your voice, make a choice
to unlock all secrets hidden,
and remember: what you refuse to ask for
can't be given.

So dare to speak your mind.
State your claim and be kind.
You'll find that things become clearer
when you take time to clear the air.
Even if you refuse to acknowledge the truth,

it's always there.
Moving forward, just beware—
of the danger of silence.

THE STREETS
Talk

From the street's deepest craters,
God curated something greater.
He created a grand human being
constructed out of sturdy stones, gravel and things.
Forming a solidified structure.
Plundering all of the dirt beneath the pavement
to procure the promise in my eyes
using the uneven surfaces to create purpose in my steps.
Stomping and exerting my strength
never wavering on the ground floor of my gifts
in pursuit of the paradise that this path produces,
my feet land the smoothest, like I was made to do this—
to use these cracks to extract wisdom.
The mission is not just discovering your talents
but implementing them—
using wet concrete to sketch your legacy into the ground beneath
so that when you're no longer around
people can still ground themselves
and stand beside your words.
Remember: the street's loudest victim is a voice unheard!

A NEW
Thing

I did a thing,
even though I was nervous and shaking,
determined not to let my fears overtake me.
Instead, I made a choice to use my voice
as a means for others to relate to me.

I used the loud inner critic
that has become an instrument,
playing tracks in my mind,
to find my motivation and rhythm.

And as the words released themselves in my mind,
I was able to be vulnerable in real time,
finding my groove.
No longer afraid to move by the beat of my own drum,
I had become an artist.
Overcoming a fear that needed to be harnessed
seemed like it would be the hardest thing for me to do.

However, I am walking away
with a new sense of accomplishment,
because how can anyone appreciate your gifts
if you keep them bottled in?

So today, I encourage you all
to begin a new thing!

FEAR'S
Fire

This year, I'll be writing my fears down on paper,
crumbling them up into a ball and getting a shot off,
tossing them all into the trash.

On second thought, as I walk past,
I'll stop to light a fire to the top of the pile,
spreading a huge smile across my face—
one that takes the place fear once occupied.

Water begins to fill my eyes, and my cheekbones will rise
as I recognize relief,
exhaling the biggest sigh
as the heat continues to rise.

However, I won't be satisfied
unless every flame demolishes my fears by name,
and I can feel myself become lighter.
Only then will I put out the fire
because I understand that as humans
we require a healthy balance of emotions.

It's just that this one has got me engulfed,
swallowing my dreams and motivation.
So before I become any more complacent,
I have to take action.

I yearn to hear the fire crackling in my ears,
sweltering up years of self-inflicted terror.

The more it burns, the merrier I'll be.
This way, I'll be free from this feeling that has bound me,
completely out of this state of stagnation.

Then I'll light a match
and burn any residual patches,
finally moving past this crippling sensation—
sending fear away on vacation
or better yet, evicting it from my mental property.

It's held me back for far too long
to continue to occupy a spot in me.
It's time to be me openly, unapologetically and unequivocally—
live boldly in my unique expression.

Today's most valuable lesson
is to recognize that we are so much better
than the internal meddling fear creates.
I encourage you all to join me
as I set that shit on fire and free up my plate!

Don't let fear stop you from making the necessary changes in your life. Never hand your power over to a feeling. Remember, you control your emotions, so don't give them room to control you. Fear was never meant to silence your voice or shatter your dreams. Walk boldly into your purpose, even if it scares you.

Fear is not meant to paralyze you. It's a cautionary emotion that serves as a means to alert you. See it as an opportunity to examine people, decisions, and changes that stand to shape your life. Allow yourself to process the emotion as it moves through you. On the other side of fear, you may find empowerment, pride, and self-actualization.

Ask yourself: What role is fear playing in my life? Is fear preventing me from reaching my purpose, or investing in a new thing? If you were to redefine fear, how would you define it?

_____

_____

_____

_____

_____

_____

_____

_____

_____

_____

Chapter VII:
SPIRITUAL ALIGNMENT

THE
Healer

Love, above all, is a call from God.
As our center and our rod, He wants us to be a reflection.
We possess all that we need, for our forgiveness is the seed
of His resurrection, and with the ability to reach one another,
we are all model specimens, called to deliver His message—
nonetheless, reflections of our brother.

Survival looks bleak without each other,
and in the event that we blunder, He helps us recover
and continues to hold our hands
with patience that withstand limits,
a fruitful love never-ending.

In Him all things are possible,
but you've got to stay the course.
However, as you step forth, you will stumble;
there will be no holding hardships from you,
they build you and become your strength.

So long as you remember who you're walking with.
Daily, you are graced with a new gift to go on.
Even if you find yourself on the wrong path,
remember that walk will not be your last;
because trouble doesn't last, and alas, God has a plan.

Love is faith that surpasses understanding;
nowhere else can we find this type of relationship—
a commitment that is too great to play with.
Jesus is the balm that I'm staying with.

I am bringing this book to a close with the Gospel of Christ. I implore you to lean into your spiritual practice of choice and find solace in the connection between you and your creator. My faith is such a pillar in my life and has helped me climb out of many difficulties. Whether you choose to follow religion or ritual, connect with a greater, loving power. Strength can be channeled through spirituality.

Take a moment to write down spiritual practices that you have, or can begin, to cover yourself in peace.

_____

_____

_____

_____

_____

_____

_____

_____

_____

_____

_____

_____

_____

_____

_____

ACKNOWLEDGEMENTS

Terry

Your ears have served as the sole recipient of my poetry for many years, long before I had the confidence to present my poems on stage and before I believed in the power of my gift. Thank you for believing in me, attentively listening to me, and recognizing the promise in my passion. You have been a solid source of motivation along this journey and countless others. I am exceedingly grateful for your continued love, encouragement, and enthusiasm. Your presence means the world to me. Thank you for standing beside me, cheering me on, working as my personal photographer and videographer, and being there to support me as I step forward to bring this long-sought passion to fruition. You will always have my love beyond measure!

Mom

As a mother, I have a deeper appreciation for your well-intentioned efforts to encourage me to pursue poetry. Some of my fondest memories with you involve your willingness to indulge my interest. Today, this is apparent in our insightful conversations. I am blessed to have a mother who has never shied away from dialogue. That open communication shaped my desire to think freely. As a child, I remember you encouraging me to enter that poetry contest, and I won! I also recall you taking me to a local stage in Berkeley to perform. I was nervous, but your presence helped calm me. Thank you for being who you are, for sharing your wisdom so freely, and for loving me and my entire family the way you do.

Lauren

I am honored that you trusted my vision enough to extend your services. I am big on being selective about what I put my name on. With that said, my appreciation of your choice to work with me on the editing aspect of this project is valued. Your professionalism and expertise are unmatched. I can't thank you enough for helping me to confidently present this project to the world.

Thank you for giving life to my work through your artistic eye. The visuals (digital art) in this book emits the elegance and emotion I intended. You followed the elements of my vision to a T and for that I appreciate you. You are a phenomenal human, and I am blessed to be your mother. I will always be proud of you! I will continue to cheer you on with excitement as you follow your promising path forward. I pray that you have a fruitful and bountiful future. I am forever grateful that you chose to join in on the creative aspect of my project. My heart is full, and I love you!

ABOUT THE AUTHOR

Alexis Monique
AM Poetry Productions
ampoetryproductions@gmail.com
Instagram: @ampoetryproductions
www.linktr.ee/ampoetryproductions

Alexis is a woman of God who leads her life from a foundation of spiritual, ethical, and moral values. As a mother of two and a wife of eighteen years, she places her family at the center of her heart and world. Education, hard work, commitment, and respect, are core values in her home.

As a native of Oakland, California, Alexis finds joy in writing and creative expression. The release of *SOAP: A Cleansing of the Soul and a Bath of Self-Realization* marks the beginning of her journey in written publication.

She holds an Associate of Arts in Communication Studies from the College of Alameda and a Bachelor of Arts in Leadership and Organizational Studies from Saint Mary's College of California. As a business professional, she has spent most of her career focused on operations, office management, budgeting, and finance.

Outside of work, Alexis nurtures her inner artist through writing poetry, and performing at spoken-word events. She finds inspiration across the spectrum of the arts, and is drawn to dance, visual art, theatre, literature, and music. Alexis has a deep-seated appreciation for diversity and the complexities of humanity. Her passions include social justice, women's empowerment, and mental wellness.

www.ingramcontent.com/pod-product-compliance
Lightning Source LLC
Chambersburg PA
CBHW020644130626
46552CB00003B/1391